Star SCENE

WHAT'S IN THE STARS
FOR ALL

EMMA

HILARY

JOSH

By Michael Anne Johns

SCHOLASTIC INC.

New York   Toronto   London   Auckland   Sydney
Mexico City   New Delhi   Hong Kong   Buenos Aires

TABLE OF CONTENTS

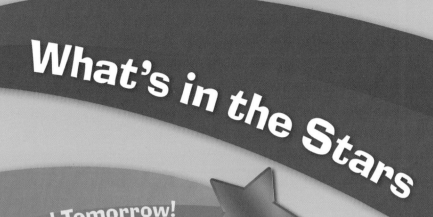

What's in the Stars

Your Faves of Today and Tomorrow!

Zac Efron, Ashley Tisdale, Corbin Bleu, Miley Cyrus . . .

unless you've been living on a mountaintop with no satellite dish, cell phone, or Internet, **everyone knows who these stars are!**

These performers are just about to take the next big step in their careers . . . and in making their moves, they will make room for the next generation of fan favorites. But who will they be? Well, *Star Scene* did an extensive search for the **new stars on the horizon** and we came up with some pretty "kewl" suggestions.

Check them out and see if you agree with our predictions of who will be next year's major rave-faves and up-and-comers!

MILEY CYRUS

Ever since Ms. Miley Cyrus arrived in Hollywood in 2006, it's been a whirlwind for the teenage singer/actress. She went from her circle of life-long friends back home in Nashville to the hustle and bustle and glam and glitter of Hollywood. She traded in her school cheerleading pom-poms for the *Hannah Montana* blond wig and wardrobe. As a matter of fact, *Hannah Montana* became the top series on the Disney Channel, and when they released the soundtrack, with nine Miley songs, it immediately hit the *Billboard* Top 200 Album chart as number one! Next, Miley hit the road with a national tour, appearing onstage at various times with the other Disney superstars, the *High School Musical* kids, the Cheetah Girls, and the Jonas Brothers! After Miley crisscrossed the United States, she headed "across the pond" [read: the Atlantic Ocean], and performed in England where her CD had also gone to the top of the charts!

When she returned home to Nashville, Miley admitted, she went to a department store to check out the *Hannah Montana* clothing line. "I tried on all the *Hannah Montana* stuff," she laughed to a reporter. "I said [to myself], 'This is weird. I'm wearing my face!'"

All of this led up to the summer 2007 release of Miley's debut solo CD, aptly named *Hannah Montana 2: Best of Both Worlds* — it included songs from *Hannah Montana* as well as her own songs.

You might say that 2007 was The Year of Miley, but what about her next move? Well, that's easy — more *Hannah Montana*, more CDs and tours, and a big leap from her TV series to movies!

It's gone from a whirlwind to a tornado for Miley, but don't worry, this is one country girl who is not going to change. "I'm not letting any stupid decisions get in my way," she insists. "I want to be a role model, letting girls know that they can follow their dreams."

"When I was little, I would stand up on couches and say, 'Watch me!' We had these showers that are completely glass, and I would lock people in them and make them stay in there and watch me perform. I'd make them watch!"

"I've always loved singing, and I've always loved acting and dancing."

Fast Fax

Real name: Destiny Hope Cyrus

Nickname: Smiley

B-day: November 23, 1992

Birthplace: Nashville, TN

Fave sport: Cheerleading

Fave car: A truck

Fave food: Raw chocolate chip cookie dough

Fave on-set snack: Candy — "I live on gummy bears and peach rings."

ZAC EFRON

You may have first noticed Zac Efron when he co-starred with teen heartthrob Jesse McCartney in the TV series, *Summerland*. But it was his first close-up in the Disney Channel mega-hit, *High School Musical* that caused a Zac Attack heard 'round the world!

Determined to use that success as a springboard for the rest of his career, Zac signed on for the *HSM* sequel, *High School Musical 2: Sing It All or Nothing!*, co-starred in the 2007 summer hit *Hairspray*, and was considered for a role in the 2008 movie *Speed Racer*. Zac has indicated he probably won't join his *HSM* cast for the threequel, which was announced as a feature film for fall 2008 and was originally called *Haunted High School Musical*.

"I just consider myself a 'working actor,'" explains Zac. "I am not trying to be a 'movie star.' I just want to get to work in my field, stretch myself, and be happy. I am not materialistic — this is not about money for me at all. I also feel like I am making my own unique contribution to this industry. I have read that I am somewhat of a 'teen idol,' but I see myself more of as a 'character actor,' to tell you the truth!"

Zac's *Hairspray* director/choreographer, Adam Shankman, agrees with him — "Bigger things are waiting for him. He is a real actor, and he gives a real performance in [*Hairspray*]."

Today & Tomorrow

"Personally, I would love to finish college and hopefully by then work in the entertainment industry whether it is acting, directing, or producing — I always want to be a part of this business, no matter what I do in it!"

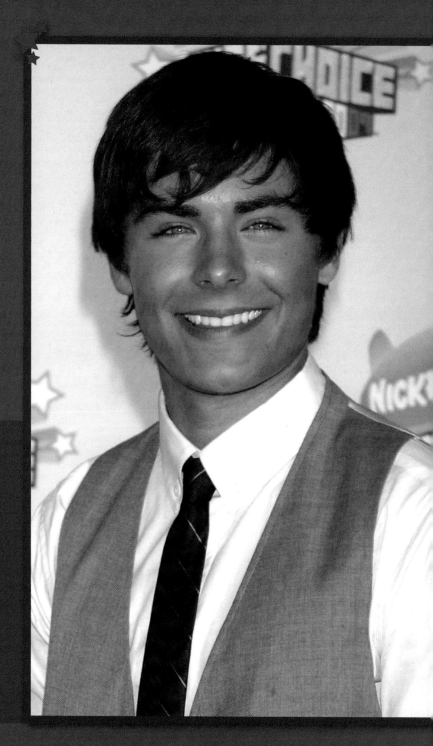

Quick Quips

What's in your pockets?
"My cell phone, an old *American Idol* wristband, and some cookie crumbs . . ."

What's the first thing you reach for in the refrigerator?
"Milk — or the Hershey's syrup (whatever is closer)."

What's your favorite holiday?
"Christmas — Santa likes my cookies."

Bindi Irwin even giggles with a delightful Down Under accent — and the nine-year-old giggles a lot. It's good to hear the blond cutie with a smile as bright as sunshine laugh, because at her young age she's already had a lifetime of sadness.

In 2006 her famous and much-loved dad, Crocodile Hunter Steve Irwin, died on location while shooting a new documentary. Days later, at Steve's memorial service, Bindi proved she was daddy's little girl when she gave a heartfelt tribute to him. And it was there she said she was going to carry on Steve Irwin's work and spread his motto, "Don't be afraid of animals."

In June of 2007 Bindi did just that when she debuted as the host of her own TV series on the Discovery Kids channel, *Bindi: The Jungle Girl*. On the series, Bindi introduces her audience to amazing animals such as koala bears, elephants, snakes, and many more. While she explains the animals' lifestyles and natural habitats, she echoes her dad's message that these creatures need our respect and protection. Because some of the show was shot before Steve Irwin passed away, he will also be seen in the series.

Bindi also appeared in an Animal Planet documentary dedicated to Steve Irwin called *My Daddy the Croc Hunter*. She is determined to continue her father's work for the rest of her life.

"Don't be afraid of animals."

One-on-One with Bindi

What can all kids do to help protect wildlife?
"Everyone can help by not buying any [protected] wildlife products."

What do you hope to accomplish with your show, *Bindi: The Jungle Girl*?
"I hope everyone learns to love all wildlife as much as my dad."

How difficult was it finishing the show without your dad?
"My dad is in every episode and we had so much fun working together!"

What do you like best about taking your dad's message to people all around the world?
"It's very cool because everyone's cheering, and it feels really nice to get out there and just be me and do what I love to do. It's really hard to explain, but it's a great feeling."

What's the biggest difference between the United States and Australia?
"There's way less kangaroos."

Why was your dad special?
"My daddy was my hero — he was always there for me when I needed him. He listened to me and taught me so many things, but most of all, he was fun."

Fast Facts

Name: Bindi Sue Irwin
B-day: July 24, 1998
Birthplace: Nambour, Queensland, Australia
Parents: Terri and the late Steve Irwin
Sibling: Younger brother Robert (Bob) Irwin

CORBIN BLEU

High School Musical, Flight 29 Down, Jump In!, High School Musical 2, his debut CD, Another Side . . . Corbin Bleu has been working on back-to-back projects for the past two years. And things aren't going to change. When he hasn't been on a set, or in a recording studio, or touring for HSM or his CD, Corbin has been looking over script after script. So, for you true-Bleu fans, expect to see Corbin in a TV series or a TV movie or a feature film — or ALL of the above — in 2008!

Complete Corbin Checklist

Name: Corbin Bleu Reivers

Stage Name: Corbin Bleu

Nickname: Bleuman, Bullet (His mom wanted to name him "Bullet Bleu.")

B-day: February 21, 1989

Birthplace: Brooklyn, NY

Righty or lefty: Right-handed

Hair: Brown

Eyes: Brown

Parents: David and Martha Reivers — his dad is an actor.

Siblings: Younger sisters Hunter, Phoenix, and Jag

First Professional Jobs: Print ads for Macy's, The Gap, Target, and Toys R Us. Fashion spreads in *Child, Parent,* and *American Baby* magazines — he started when he was a toddler.

First Concert: Weird Al

First Book Read: *The Happy Hocky Family* by Lane Smith

Education: Los Angeles County High School for the Arts; Corbin was also one of the first students at the prestigious Debbie Allen Dance Academy.

Collection: Belt buckles

Fave Sport: Basketball

Fave Musicians: Prince, Michael Jackson, Lenny Kravitz, Justin Timberlake

Fave Female Singer: Beyoncé

Fave Car: Porsche Spider

Fave Fast Food: In-N-Out

Fave Drink: Lemonade

Fave Candy: Twix bar

Fave Sandwich: Sausage and peppers

Fave Ice Cream: Cold Stone's Cake Batter

Fave Chewing Gum: Eclipse Spearmint

Fave Holiday: Christmas

Fave Colors: Gold and black

Fave School Subject: Science

Fave Book: *The Great Gatsby* by F. Scott Fitzgerald

Fave Author: J. K. Rowling

Fave Historical Era: The 1980s — "because I love the music, fashion, and hair."

Fave Board Game: Trouble

Fave Actress: Jennifer Garner and Angelina Jolie

Résumé

Films

High School Musical 2: Sing It All or Nothing! (2007)

Flight 29 Down: The Movie (2007)

Jump In! (2007)

High School Musical (2006)

Catch That Kid (2004)

Galaxy Quest (1999)

Family Tree (1999)

Beach Movie (1999)

Soldier (1998)

Albums

High School Musical 2 soundtrack (2007)

Another Side (2007)

Jump In! soundtrack (2007)

High School Musical soundtrack (2006)

Disneymania Volume 4 (2006)

"There are a lot of projects in the works right now that aren't quite set in stone yet. What would be ideal for me would be to continue doing features, go work on Broadway, and then go on a worldwide tour for another album. I want to do it all."

ASHLEY TISDALE

Like her *HSM* buddies Corbin and Zac, Ashley has been busy, busy, busy with nonstop work. After *High School Musical*, Ashley returned to her Disney Channel series, *The Suite Life of Zack and Cody*, reprised her role of Sharpay in *High School Musical 2: Sing It All or Nothing!*, and even found time to fit in recording her debut CD, *Headstrong*. She, too, is considering a regular TV sitcom and signing on the dotted line for a feature film!

Needless to say, Ashley is the center of attention wherever she goes. She is asked so many questions all the time, that Ashley can practically finish any sentence she hears. We put together some of 'em!

Tisdale Tid-bits

My dog's name is . . .
"Blondie, which is my nickname on *The Suite Life of Zack and Cody*."

My most prized possession is . . .
"my Louis Vuitton bag."

When my friends come over . . .
"we love to watch movies."

Yes, I'm a natural curly brunette, but . . .
"I love change, and I love changing my hair."

Some people think . . .
"acting is so glamorous, but it's hard work and 90 percent rejection."

The best advice I ever got is . . .
"if you want something, work for it."

My favorite family tradition is . . .
"to watch *Miracle on 34th Street* during Thanksgiving."

My biggest childhood fear was . . .
"Santa Claus — I didn't like the idea of someone coming into my house when I was sleeping."

The cereal in my kitchen cupboard is . . .
"peanut butter Cap'n Crunch."

During high school I made extra money working at . . .
"the mall, because my parents really wanted me to have that normal experience of a regular job. I think it was a great thing to do. I worked at Abercrombie & Fitch, Hollister, Wet Seal, and Windsor. Back then, I hated it. I had to clean up after shoppers — like scraping gum off the floor — so it was definitely a reality check for me."

I'm not part of the Hollywood scene because . . .
"I'm not really comfortable in situations at parties and stuff."

My early experiences were good for me because . . .
"I'm glad I took this road, where I was struggling at first . . . now I don't take anything for granted."

SELENA GOMEZ

If the popularity of the Disney channel's *Wizards of Waverly Place* is any indication, the cast: Jake T. Austin, Selena Gomez, Jennifer Stone, and David Henrie are going to be the superstars of tomorrow!

Fast Fax

Name: Selena Marie Gomez
***Wizards* Character:** Alex
B-day: July 22, 1992

On Her Character, Alex:
"Alex is very funky and energetic and outgoing. She's a bit mischievous. Actually, she's probably the most mischievous one out of the whole family . . . I like her. She's very cool."

On Alex's Magical Powers:
"She can do duplication spells, and there might be some flying objects and stuff like that."

If She Had Magical Powers in Real Life:
"I would like to zap food anywhere and at any time — pizza or shrimp scampi."

On Her Favorite School Subject:
"Science, at the moment. I'm studying physical science — the layers of the earth and everything. I think it's fascinating to learn about our earth."

Waverly Place

Name: David Clayton Henrie
Nickname: Dave
***Wizards* Character:** Sully
B-day: July 11, 1989
Birthplace: Los Angeles, CA
Right or Lefty: left-handed
Instrument: Guitar
Hair: Brown
Eyes: Green
Fave Movies: *Godfather 1, 2, 3; Raging Bull, Rebel Without a Cause*
Fave Actress: Meryl Streep
Fave Actors: Jim Carrey, Al Pacino, Robert DeNiro
Fave Musicians: Jimi Hendrix, Axl Rose

Fave Car: 1969 Camero, 1967 Impala, or 1969 Cadillac
Fave Food: Steak
Fave Drink: Water
Fave Sandwich: Chicken
Fave Ice Cream: Frozen yogurt
Fave Holiday: Christmas
Fave Color: Red
Fave School Subject: History

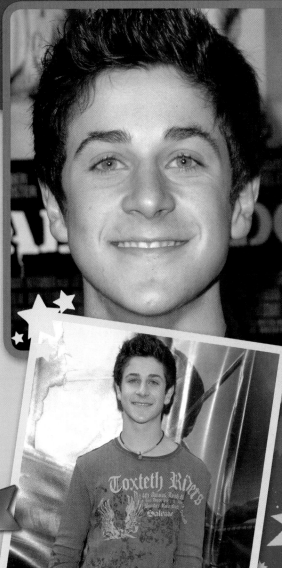

Name: Jennifer Stone
***Wizards* Character:** Harper
B-day: February 12, 1993
Birthplace: Arlington, TX
Right or Lefty: Right-handed
Hair: Auburn
Eyes: Dark brown

Fave TV Show: *Boy Meets World*
Fave Movie: *Breakfast at Tiffany's*
Fave Actress: Meryl Streep
Fave Car: 1964 Mustang
Fave Food: Cookie dough

Fave Fast Food Restaurant: Chick-Fil-A
Fave Drink: Water
Fave Candy: Reese's Pieces
Fave Ice Cream: Cookie dough

Fave Designers: Chanel, Anna Sui
Fave Holiday: Christmas
Fave Color: Purple
Fave Book: *Blink* by Malcolm Gladwell
Fave Author: Jane Austen

JAKE T. AUSTIN

Just Jake

Jake was born on December 3, 1994

His hometown is New York, NY

Jake's real name is Jake Toranzo Szymanski

Jakes is a huge Yankees fan – "I've been one all my life!"

Being a Yankee fan made it double fun for him to play the voice of Yankee Irving in the film *Everyone's Hero*. That was the last film the late Christopher Reeve directed and produced.

Jake plays Max in *Wizards of Waverly Place*.

Jakes has also appeared in the Disney Channel movie *Johnny Kapahala: Back on Board*, as Chris; *The Perfect Game*; the voice of Nicky in *Ant Bully*; and the voice of Diego in the series, *Go, Diego! Go!*

EMMA ROBERTS

Emma Roberts is part of Hollywood royalty — both personally and professionally! First of all, she is the daughter of actor Eric Roberts and the niece of actress Julia Roberts.

That alone puts a tiara on her head! And the shining diamond in that crown is the fact that Emma has become the face and voice of one of America's original teen queens, Nancy Drew!

In the summer of 2007, Emma, who had already won the hearts of 'tweens all over as Addie Singer of Nickelodeon's series, *Unfabulous*, starred in the modern-day version of the classic adaptation of *Nancy Drew*. The film was such a hit, there is talk that Emma will take on the role of the super sleuth once again for a sequel! No wonder Emma was voted the Female Star of Tomorrow at the ShoWest Convention in 2007!

How are you like Nancy Drew?
"I can be a perfectionist, and I appreciate her sense of humor. I haven't solved any mysteries of my own, but maybe I'll stumble across one sometime! . . . Actually, Nancy is kind of the opposite of me because she's a complete, complete perfectionist. I mean, I'm a perfectionist with some things, but not to the point she is. And she's much more proper and well-mannered, I guess you could say [laughs]."

Was it scary to play such a classic character?
"Yes. Everyone has their own perception of the character from reading the books, so I don't know if they'll like the way I play her."

When did you first start acting?
"I was an extra on the set of my aunt's movie *America's Sweetheart*. That's when I really wanted to start [acting]."

Where's your favorite city to shop?
"New York City, of course! [I love] all the little boutiques they have around there — they are really cute."

Have you asked your aunt or your dad for career advice?
"I really haven't. I think people assume that just because we're all in the business, we talk about it all the time. But I never really talk about it with them. I think the best advice you can get is what you learn yourself when you're on the set and [from what] you observe. I've learned from experience."

Fun Fax

- Emma loves to dip the crust of pizza in ranch dressing!
- Emma's favorite jeans are True Religion and Miss Sixty.
- Before she started home-schooling, Emma went to Archer School for Girls in Brentwood, CA.
- Emma loves her TiVo — she never misses taping *Lost* or *America's Next Top Model*.
- Emma always carries her Blackberry.
- Emma's favorite fast food restaurant is In-N-Out.

Emma's Space

Is it true you want to go to college at New York University?
"Yes! I love New York so much. I want to study photography. I also love fashion design. . . . College is still [a little way off], but I would love to go to NYU. I have some other places in mind, but I would really like to go there."

Who is the coolest person you have worked with?
"I've worked with so many great people but I really liked Johnny Depp. He is just a really nice guy. He's really great. I would love to work with him again in the future."

Is there a book or book series — besides Nancy Drew — you really like?
"Probably the *Gossip Girl* series and *Staying Fat for Sarah Byrnes* . . . I also really like *My Sister's Keeper*."

CHRIS BROWN

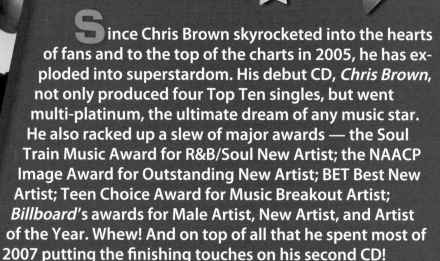

Since Chris Brown skyrocketed into the hearts of fans and to the top of the charts in 2005, he has exploded into superstardom. His debut CD, *Chris Brown*, not only produced four Top Ten singles, but went multi-platinum, the ultimate dream of any music star. He also racked up a slew of major awards — the Soul Train Music Award for R&B/Soul New Artist; the NAACP Image Award for Outstanding New Artist; BET Best New Artist; Teen Choice Award for Music Breakout Artist; *Billboard*'s awards for Male Artist, New Artist, and Artist of the Year. Whew! And on top of all that he spent most of 2007 putting the finishing touches on his second CD!

But Chris isn't stopping at conquering just the music world — he's started flexing his talent in the acting arena, too. He guested on the TV series, *One on One*, had a recurring role on *The O.C.*, appeared in the films *Stomp the Yard*, *After School*, *This Christmas*, and the upcoming *Phenom*.

On top of it all, Chris is Mr. Charisma. He's always got something interesting to say . . . so you're invited to take a peek at his top "Five."

Fast Fax

Name: Christopher Maurice Brown

B-day: May 5, 1989

Birthplace: Tappahannock, VA

Fave Car: Range Rover

Fave School Subject: Math

Fave Books: *Harry Potter* series

1 "My biggest insecurity is my height. I'm 6'1". If I get too tall, it'll be hard to dance because there's so much more to do to move your body!"

2 "I'm kinda surprised [at my success]. It's overwhelming and humbling. It's a blessing. I just thank God as well as my family, my people around me, my management, my mom – everybody keeps me grounded."

3 "I'm still a kid, so I'm going to do kid things. I'm going to have my games. I'm going to make sure I'm surrounded by that kind of activity. . . . I have a basketball court on the [tour] bus. I put it in a trailer, and it's a portable one, so we just hook it up wherever we want to play."

4 "Fans . . . just come up to me. I'll speak to you, no problem. I'm the same down-to-earth kind of guy. I'm not going to change for anybody."

5 "I'm not one to argue. I just leave the room, 'cause people can't argue by themselves!"

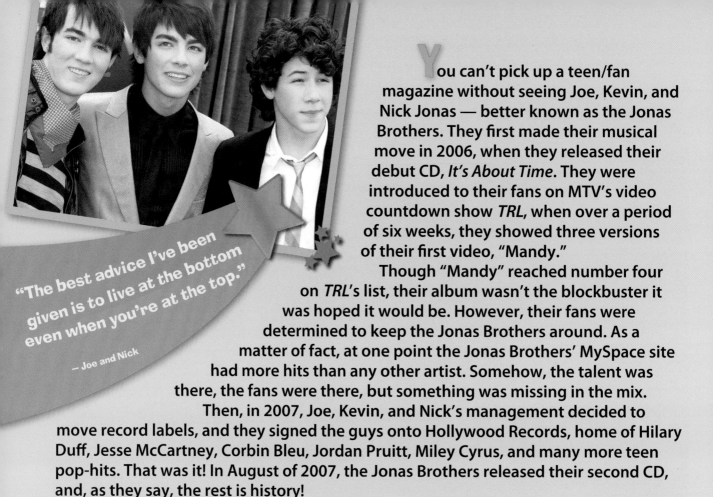

You can't pick up a teen/fan magazine without seeing Joe, Kevin, and Nick Jonas — better known as the Jonas Brothers. They first made their musical move in 2006, when they released their debut CD, *It's About Time*. They were introduced to their fans on MTV's video countdown show *TRL*, when over a period of six weeks, they showed three versions of their first video, "Mandy."

Though "Mandy" reached number four on *TRL*'s list, their album wasn't the blockbuster it was hoped it would be. However, their fans were determined to keep the Jonas Brothers around. As a matter of fact, at one point the Jonas Brothers' MySpace site had more hits than any other artist. Somehow, the talent was there, the fans were there, but something was missing in the mix. Then, in 2007, Joe, Kevin, and Nick's management decided to move record labels, and they signed the guys onto Hollywood Records, home of Hilary Duff, Jesse McCartney, Corbin Bleu, Jordan Pruitt, Miley Cyrus, and many more teen pop-hits. That was it! In August of 2007, the Jonas Brothers released their second CD, and, as they say, the rest is history!

"The best advice I've been given is to live at the bottom even when you're at the top."
— Joe and Nick

"The best advice I got is to stay true to who you are."
— Kevin

Jonas Brothers: The Juicy Stuff

- In 2007, at a Diabetes Research Institute event, Nick revealed he has Type 1 Diabetes, so he could be a spokesperson to educate kids about the disease. He found out he had the disease in 2005 when the group was on tour in Europe.
- Kevin and Joe's best friend is from their hometown in New Jersey — his nickname is "Joey Baga Donuts"!
- One of Nick's best friends is Mandy, the girl they wrote the song "Mandy" about.
- Nick is a major New York Yankees fan.

- Kevin's favorite place in the world is Indonesia.
- When Joe opens the refrigerator, the first thing he reaches for is Gatorade.
- Joe's favorite holiday is Thanksgiving "because of all the good food."
- Kevin's favorite holiday is Christmas — "It's the best."
- Nick's favorite holiday is Christmas "because it's fun to get presents."

SARA PAXTON

California girl Sara Paxton is definitely on the high road to success. She's steadily gained popularity with fans via her TV work on the series, *Darcy's Wild Life* and *Summerland*, and in the feature films *Sleepover*, *Aquamarine*, and the upcoming *Sydney White*. She sang on the *Darcy's Wild Life* soundtrack and is considering releasing a CD of her own in the near future.

Want to know more about Sara? Well here are six must-know facts about her . . .

1 Sara was born on April 25, 1988 in Woodland Hills, CA.

2 Sara's mom is from Mexico, and the young actress loves her Hispanic heritage. "Everything we do is really family oriented and everyone loves to party," she says. "I think that comes along with being Hispanic. Everyone's loud and constantly dancing!"

3 Sara's favorite animals on *Darcy's Wild Life* were a pig and a chimpanzee. "The pig was so smart," she says. "Whenever somebody sneezed, it would run and get a tissue." And the chimp — "They are so smart. It's like you're talking to a little person and not an animal. They can understand everything you're saying."

4 Maui, Hawaii, is Sara's favorite retreat. "I go there every summer after school ends with my family," she says. "It's so beautiful."

5 Sara played Jesse McCartney's girlfriend on *Summerland*. "It was great," she recalls. "He was really nice. It was cool because I got to play his girlfriend, and all my friends were jealous. It was really funny."

6 Sara is proud of being a role model. "I'm just a normal teenager. I guess I won't be wearing skimpy outfits if eight year olds are looking up to me, but I wouldn't be wearing that anyways."

On being compared to Hilary Duff . . .
"I think it's really nice. I mean Hilary's had an amazing career, and I think it's a compliment. I hope that I can be as successful as she is, but we're definitely different, you know?"

Heroes

Everyone wants to be a hero . . . to save the world or even just a neighborhood! Well, Masi Oka and Hayden Panettiere get to do just that in the must-see hit TV series *Heroes*.

When the show first started in 2006, no one expected *Heroes* to become one of the most popular shows on television. Needless to say since then, the *Heroes* cast cause paparazzi flashbulbs to pop every time they make an appearance . . . on a red carpet or at the local grocery store!

Masi Oka, who plays Hiro Nakamura, and Hayden Panettiere, who plays cheerleader Claire Bennet on *Heroes*, are fan-favorites. Let's put them under the spotlight . . . .

> "Everything begins with believing. It's like that song from Prince of Egypt, 'There can be miracles when you believe.'"
> — Masi

Masi Must-Knows

- His name is Masayori "Masi" Oka, and he was born December 27, 1974, in Tokyo, Japan.

- Masi is a math whiz! He graduated from Brown University with a Bachelor of Science degree in computer science and mathematics. He has a 180-plus IQ.

- Masi speaks Japanese, English, German, and Spanish.

- In 1987, when he was 12 years old, Masi appeared on the cover of *Time* magazine for the article, "Those Asian-American Whiz Kids."

- His favorite hobby is Kendo, which is Japanese sword fighting.

- If he could pick a super power for himself, he says, "I would probably pick time travel."

- Masi worked for director/producer George Lucas's special effects company Industrial Light & Magic — he developed a computer program to create water effects that was used in the films, *A Perfect Storm* and *Pirates of the Caribbean*. He still consults with ILM.

- Masi loves to tell everyone of his ability to make drum beats and turntable scratching sounds with his mouth. "I can beatbox!" he exclaims.

- During his 2007 hiatus, Masi made the 2008 film *Get Smart*.

- Steve Carell of the TV series, *The Office*, is one of his favorite actors.

HAYDEN PANETTIERE

Heroine Hayden

- Hayden released a CD for Hollywood Records in 2007.
- She had singles on the soundtracks of *Ice Princess* and *Tiger Cruise*.
- Hayden's dad is a retired lieutenant in the New York City Fire Department.
- Hayden's first professional job was when she was 11 months old and she did a Playskool commercial.
- When she was seven, Hayden had landed the role of Lizzie Spaulding on the soap opera, *Guiding Light*.
- Hayden is involved with an organization called Whaleman Foundation — "It raises awareness about whaling and sea life, how damaging it is, and how they are being killed."
- Hayden's first car was a Porsche Cayenne Sport — her first big purchase!
- If Hayden could have a super power it would be teleporting — "That way, I could be talking to you right now from Fiji or Tahiti or Thailand."
- Hayden's BFF is Rumer Willis, the eldest daughter of Bruce Willis and Demi Moore.
- Hayden stars in the 2008 film, *Fireflies in the Garden*.
- Hayden was signed as a cover girl for an international ad campaign for Neutrogena.

KYLE MASSEY

Atlanta-native Kyle Massey was born to be a star! He's been acting since he was in elementary school, but it was when the 12-year-old Kyle was tapped for the Cory role on Disney Channel's *That's So Raven* that his career really took off. Kyle appeared in more than 100 episodes of the hit series, and when it finally went off the air, he was asked to star in the spin-off series, *Cory in the House*. Of course, his answer was "YES!" Set in the White House — Cory's dad has been hired as the chef for the president of the United States — *Cory in the House* became one of the network's top-rated shows as soon as it premiered.

Kyle's A-list

- "If I were president, the first law I would pass would be National No School Week! You'd get an extra week of summer vacation."

- "I got to meet Tiger Woods. . . . Meeting him was one of my favorite moments and a real honor. Whenever I set foot on the golf course, I want to be like Tiger."

- "I love reading . . . believe it or not, it can save your life. If you try to go onto a highway and you don't know how to read and the sign says 'Don't Walk,' your life can possibly be in danger. So reading is very, very important in life."

- "In ten years I see myself opening some type of business. I haven't quite narrowed it down yet, but something is coming. Or owning a few pieces of real estate that generate revenue for me and create a fun, safe place for kids to hang out and have fun. Kinda Donald Trump-ish for kids, I hope!"

Quickies

- Before he goes to bed, Kyle "prays and drinks a bottle of water."
- Kyle thinks Christina Milian is really cute!
- "Fingernails on a chalk board really annoy me."
- "I would love to co-star in a movie with Martin Lawrence, Will Smith, and Jim Carrey."
- "If I were an animal, I would be a dog."
- "My favorite midnight snack is pineapples."

SHIA LABEOUF

In 2007 the powers-that-be of Hollywood moviemakers got together in Las Vegas for their annual film preview/prediction convention called ShoWest. In addition to films, certain stars were singled out for their talents and anticipated future success. Shia LaBeouf was named ShoWest's Male Star of Tomorrow. He was an obvious choice considering Shia was only 14 when he starred in the Disney Channel's *Even Stevens* — he won a Daytime Emmy in 2003 for that show — and followed it up with the films, *The Battle of Shaker Height; Charlie's Angels: Full Throttle; Dumb & Dumberer: When Harry Met Lloyd; Holes; I, Robot; The Greatest Game Ever Played; Nausicaä of the Valley of the Wind* (voice); *Constantine; Bobby; A Guide to Recognizing Your Saints; Disturbia; Transformers* (he has signed on for the sequels, too); and *Surf's Up*. Shia has also taken a role in the 2008 super-sequel, *Indiana Jones 4*.

- Shia claims his proudest moment was "when I told my mom that she did not have to go back to work because I booked my first real-money job. The studio called and said *Even Stevens* was a green light for three seasons, which meant I had a job for three years."

- Shia says the hardest part of filming *Transformers* was "the physical [part]." Explains Shia, "I worked out a lot. Not weights, but calisthenics and running for a good three months, just because [director] Michael Bay said, 'This is nonstop; it's like running a marathon.'"

- Shia's newfound fame is a bit weird for him. "You want to be recognized, you want to be in the movies," he says. "But then when it happens, it's strange because you're the same guy. And you're still not sure you deserve any of it."

- Tom Hanks is Shia's role model — "He does it all. He's got Oscars. He's loved. He can do the blockbuster. He's someone America trusts … I want to be an actor like that. I want to be someone you can trust."

- Shia loves to surf and play golf.

- *Catcher in the Rye* was Shia's favorite book when he was a kid.

Shia's

- Shia was born on June 11, 1986, in the Echo Park section of Los Angeles, CA.

- His dad, Jeffrey, was once a circus clown, and his mom, Shayna, was a ballerina.

- Jeffrey LaBeouf trained chickens for his circus act, and Shia remembers having to live with those fowl-friends living in the bathtub in their house!

- Shia attended the Hamilton Academy of Music in Los Angeles, CA, and now is taking courses at the University of the Pacific (in between projects).

It could be said that James "Lil' JJ" Lewis's life is set to a laugh track! A natural-born comedian, this Little Rock, Arkansas, native has been making people giggle-to-guffaw since he was just a little shorty! Like many legendary funny-men, JJ started out as a class clown — loved by his classmates and a thorn in the side to many of his teachers. Except there was one teacher — his physical education teacher, Ken Bright — who appreciated his humor. When JJ was hauled down to the principal's office for cutting up in class, it was usually Mr. Bright who took over. Seeing that JJ had something special, Mr. Bright encouraged him to try his comedy licks on stage. They worked on jokes together and JJ was soon performing at local comedy events . . . and bringing down the house!

Next came a BET competition — JJ won. Then a competition at the famous Apollo Theater in New York City followed — he won. JJ then landed a role in the Queen Latifah movie, *Beauty Shop* and went on to

LIL' JJ

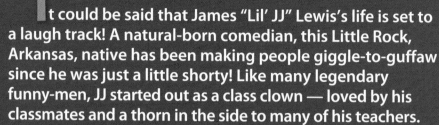

other comedy films, *Yours, Mine and Ours* and *Crossover*. All the while, Mr. Bright, who had become JJ's manager, was guiding his career.

But by far, JJ's biggest break was earning his own series on Nickelodeon's, *Just Jordan*, which premiered in January 2007.

What does the future hold for JJ? Anything he wants! "I want to do everything!" JJ says. "I want to be an all-around entertainer. I like actin' and dancin' and rappin' and singin' and performing stand-up comedy."

LOL From Lil' JJ

Name: James Charles Lewis

Nickname/Stage Name: Lil' JJ

B-day: October 31, 1990

Birthplace: Little Rock, AK

Parents: Tonya and Frazier Lewis

Siblings: Two younger brothers, one younger sister

Lefty or Righty: Right-handed

First Book Read: *Green Eggs and Ham* by Dr. Seuss

Fave Sports: Basketball, football

Fave Movie: *Rush Hour*

Fave Food: Fruit

Fave Fast Food: McDonald's

Fave Soda: Sprite

Fave Candy: Skittles

Fave Sandwich: Cheeseburger

Fave Ice Cream: Vanilla

Fave After-School Snack: Pop-Tarts

Fave Holiday: Valentine's Day

Fave Color: Red

Fave School Subject: Math

Fave Book Series: *Harry Potter*

"I consider myself a spokesperson for kids and teenagers. A lot of stuff . . . they don't know how to say it. I'm gonna say what the kids want to say. I'm gonna get it off their chest."

ABIGAIL BRESLIN

Best known for her lead role in the award-winning film, *Little Miss Sunshine*, 'tween Abigail Breslin is quickly racking up quite a résumé. And it looks as if the best is yet to come! Check out our peek at the superstar-in-training.

Name: Abigail Kathleen Breslin

Nickname: Abbie

Name Origin: Abigail was named after former First Lady of the U.S., Abigail Adams.

B-day: April 14, 1996

Birthplace: New York, NY

Siblings: Older brother, actor Spencer Breslin (they appeared in *Raising Helen* as brother and sister) and older brother Ryan

Pets: Two dogs and a cat

Awards: Nominated for a Best Supporting Actress Oscar for *Little Miss Sunshine*

Collections: American Girl dolls and stuffed animals

Fun Fact: Abigail is double-jointed.

Fave Disney Movie: *Finding Nemo*

Summer Fun: Abigail likes to go to New Jersey — "My cousins live there. I like to go to the woods and . . . catch frogs."

Secret 2006 Crush: *American Idol*'s Kevin Covais — "I cried when he got voted off. I have a doll that looks like Chicken Little, so I call it Kevin."

Fave School Subjects: Reading, art, and history

Most Exciting Moment: Wearing expensive Harry Winston jewelry at the Golden Globes Awards

Résumé

Films

Nim's Island (2008)

American Girl (2008)

Definitely, Maybe (2007)

No Reservations (2007)

The Santa Clause 3: The Escape Clause (2006)

The Ultimate Gift (2006)

Little Miss Sunshine (2006)

Air Buddies (2006)

Chestnut: Hero of Central Park (2004)

Keane (2004)

The Princess Diaries 2: Royal Engagement (2004)

Raising Helen (2004)

Signs (2002)

On Being Compared to Dakota Fanning:
"She's really good, so I take that as a compliment."

JOSH HUTCHERSON

In the past several years, it seems as if Kentucky born-'n'-bred Josh Hutcherson is in *every* movie made! No wonder this cutie is on everyone's must-watch list.

Just Josh: Everything You Ever Wanted to Know

Name: Joshua Ryan Hutcherson

Nickname: Josh or JHutch

B-day: October 12, 1992

Astro Sign: Libra

Birthplace: Union, KY

Righty or Lefty: Right-handed

Eyes: Hazel with a blue-ish tint

Hair: Light brown

Parents: Chris and Michelle Hutcherson

Sibling: Younger brother Connor

Pets: A boxer dog named Diesel, two cats named Jell-O and Paws, and a turtle

Hobby: Building RC cars — "They go 50 miles an hour! I live in suburbia so I can drive 'em down the street. I have some trucks that can off-road and do jumps!"

Scar: On his hand from an accident when he was seven years old

Schooling: Home-schooled

First Professional Job: A TV pilot called *House Blend* in 2002

First Major Purchase: A dirt bike

Fave Pastimes: Going to movies, video/DVD games like *100,000 Pyramid, Family Feud, Madden '07* for Xbox 360, *Call of Duty*

Fave Rollercoaster: Son of Beast at Kings Island theme park

Fave Type of Music: Rap and hip-hop

Fave Sports: Football, soccer, basketball, baseball, tennis

Fave Sports Team: NFL's Cincinnati Bengals

Fave Sports Player: Rudi Johnson of the Bengals

Fave Vacation Place: Atlantis Resort in Paradise Island, Bahamas

Fave Actors: Brad Pitt, Jake Gyllenhaal

Fave Actress: Angelina Jolie

Fave TV Shows: *Family Guy* and *The Andy Milonakis Show*

Fave Color: Red

Fave Book: *Eragon*

Fave School Subject: Algebra

Fave Fast Food Restaurant: Subway (honey-nut bread, turkey, pepperoni, pepperjack cheese, and lettuce sandwich)

Little Known Fact: Josh has his own production company called Jetlagged Productions.

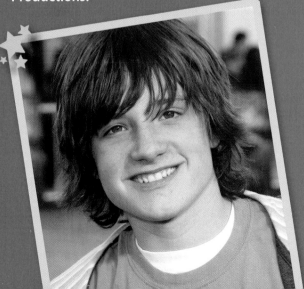

Résumé

Films

Winged Creatures (2008)

Journey 3-D (2008)

Firehouse Dog (2007)

Bridge To Terabithia (2007)

RV (2006)

Zathura: A Space Adventure (2006)

Little Manhattan (2006)

Howl's Moving Castle (voice) (2005)

Kicking & Screaming (2005)

The Courtship of Eddie's Father (2005)

The Polar Express (2004)

Motocross Kids (2004)

Wilder Days (2004)

American Splendor (2003)

Miracle Dogs (2003)

As Megan Parker on Nickelodeon's series, *Drake & Josh*, Miranda Cosgrove became the prankster, bratty little sister you loved to hate! She was constantly making life miserable for her TV brothers — and adding laughs across America!

As *Drake & Josh* was wrapping up its final season, Nickelodeon announced some big news for Miranda — she was getting her own show in the Fall of 2007. Called *iCarly*, the series is a "show-within-a-show."

Miranda is Carly, a teen who hosts her own Web show and interacts with her audience by giving the viewers "assignments" that will be included on a future show. The cool thing about *iCarly* is that real-life viewers are really part of Carly's audience, and they submit their own Web creations!

The buzz around *iCarly* is deafening and Miranda is definitely hot, hot, hot!

MIRANDA COSGROVE

The Basics

Name:
Miranda Taylor Cosgrove

B-day: May 14, 1993

Birthplace: Los Angeles, CA

Hair: Dark brown

Eyes: Brown

Pet: A dog

Instruments: Piano and guitar

Fave Place: Anywhere near the sea

Fave Actress:
Rachel McAdams

Fave Actor: Orlando Bloom

iChat With Miranda

Describe your experience on *Drake & Josh*.

"It was so much fun getting to work with Drake and Josh. I mean, they're like the two funniest guys ever, and they made me laugh every day a million times. It was really fun. Drake's all into music and dancing, so it was cool to be influenced by the music he likes. We actually did swing dancing together for a while on set, which was fun."

What do you do for fun?

"As far as sports go, I actually fence, and I horseback ride, and I play guitar, which is really fun. Basically, I just hang out with my friends and go see movies constantly. I love movies."

Did you enjoy the break between *Drake & Josh* and *iCarly*?

"Sometimes I get kind of bored if I go like a month or so and I'm not doing anything. At first I'm like, 'Cool, I'll have a little time off and I'll get to hang out with friends,' but then after a little while goes by I'm like, 'Oh,' and I really wish that I could go back and start doing work again. It's just a blast to get to come in to the set and say hi to everyone and work with people you know. After a few months it seems like everybody's like family."

What are your future goals?

"I definitely want to go to college. That's a big thing with me. I have a few friends, that we're like, already planning and we want to go to the same college, which would be really fun. I'd love to be an actor, but I'd also like to be a marine biologist."

HILARY DUFF

Duff Stuff

It's been quite a charmed road for Hilary Duff. From being crowned teen-queen when she starred in the Disney Channel top-rated series/movie franchise, *Lizzie McGuire*, to movie star, *Billboard* chart topper, fashion trendsetter, and even Barbie doll model, Hilary has already made her showbiz mark at the age of 20! Her 2007 CD, *Dignity*, was a major hit, and even while she was on tour promoting the CD, Hilary had two movies released — the animated *Foodfight!* (she was the voice of Sunshine Goodness) and *War, Inc.* Her next film, *Talking With Dog*, will come out in 2008, as will a trip back to the recording studio to work on her next CD!

On how her CD, *Dignity*, was different from her previous CDs . . .
"It is still pop, but it is very different for me. It's got some Indian vibes, Balinese beats, a little bit of hip-hop and dance-pop, so it sounds kind of '80s. It's very all over the same place. And that's my taste in music. So it was really fun for me to put all those elements together and really be a part of creating it this time around. This record is just really honest. All the things I wrote about are things that I deal with, things I want to talk about. It fits where I am in my life."

On her fragrance, Hilary Duff's "With Love" . . .
"I seriously loved making it — I'm already bugging them to make another one. I got to go to the labs and see how it works. I didn't actually *concoct* it myself, but I chose all the smells, the notes that I wanted there to be in the perfume: how warm, how sweet, or the staying power. Perfumers know everything about where the stuff came from. I learned a lot and to get to design the bottle was fun."

On Hilary's fashion line, "stuff by hilary duff" . . .
"There's a collection called Broken English, and it's lots of little plaids and little ties — like girly punk. We did really cool things — the shirt would be attached to a little sweater vest done in a cool kind of punk way."

On being part of the Hollywood set . . .
"When I go out, it's to be with friends, which is almost the same as hanging out at home. I don't go out for the scene.'"

On her first concert . . .
"I was 10, and my sister let me tag along. We saw No Doubt in Houston for the *Tragic Kingdom* tour when Gwen [Stefani] had braces and pink hair. I loved her. I always wanted braces. All the cooler older kids had braces and would match their rubber bands to their outfits."

On where she sees herself in five years . . .
"I hope to still be doing my music and acting and my fashion. I love houses and maybe would like to do some home decorating. One day I could see myself being an architect. I'm trying to learn how to cook but don't really have much time!"

THE NAKED BROTHERS BAND

The family that plays together, stays together — at least that's what the stars and creators of Nickelodeon's *The Naked Brothers Band* believe. The hot, hot, hot series was created by actress/writer/producer Polly Draper and stars not only her husband, musician/composer Michael Wolff, but their two sons, Alex and Nat Wolff. The two boys mix their real-life with reel-life and play the leaders of an all-kid rock band — something they did on their own even before the show! The on-screen group, The Naked Brothers Band, has reached superstardom, and with each new episode, it looks as if Alex and Nat are doing the same.

Alex and Nat Fab Fax

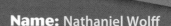

Name: Alexander Draper Wolff
B-day: November 1, 1997
Birthplace: Los Angeles, CA
Righty or lefty: Right-handed
Hair: Brown
Eyes: Brown
Sibling: Older brother, Nat
Musical Influences: Green Day, Drake Bell, Beatles
Fave Sport: Skateboarding
Fave TV Show: *Drake & Josh*
Fave Movies: *Grind*
Fave Actor: Leonardo DiCaprio
Fave Actresses: Beyoncé, Jessica Alba
Fave Food: Cheeseburger
Fave Fast Food Restaurant: In-N-Out
Fave Drink: Milk
Fave Soda: Lemon/Lime Seltzer
Fave Sandwich: PB&J
Fave Chewing Gum: Trident Splash
Fave Ice Cream: Strawberry
Fave Clothes: T-shirts
Fave Holiday: Christmas
Fave Color: Red
First Book Read: *Cat in the Hat* by Dr. Seuss

Name: Nathaniel Wolff
B-day: December 17, 1994
Birthplace: Los Angeles, CA
Righty or lefty: Left-handed (but he plays sports with his right hand)
Hair: Brown
Eyes: Green
Sibling: Younger brother, Alex
Musical Influence: Paul McCartney
Fave Sports: Basketball, Tennis
Fave TV Shows: *Friends, I Love Lucy, The O.C., Family Guy, Monk*
Fave Movie: *Harvey, Stand By Me, Ace Ventura*
Fave Actors: James Stewart, River Phoenix, Jim Carrey, James Dean
Fave Car: Mustang
Fave Food: Ice cream
Fave Fast Food: Cheeseburger
Fave Drink: Strawberry milkshake
Fave Sandwich: Roast beef
Fave Chewing Gum: Trident
Fave Ice Cream: Strawberry
Fave Clothes: T-shirts
Fave Holiday: Christmas Eve
Fave Color: Red
Fave Web Site: Google
Fave Books: *Small Steps, Holes*

How They Got Their Name:

"Mom says when I was four and Alex was one, we got out of the tub and said, 'We're the Naked Brothers Band.' But we don't think it's true."

— Nat